MATSUMOTO TORATA 松本寅太

Bojutsu
The Matsumoto System

MATSUMOTO TORATA

translated by eric shahan

Copyright © 2017 Eric Michael Shahan

All Rights Reserved.

ISBN-13: 978-1544885179

ISBN-10: 1544885172

※ other works translated by eric shahan ※

Ninjutsu

by Gingetsu Itoh

Ninjutsu to Yojutsu
Ninjutsu no Gokui
Gendaijin no Ninjutsu

Senjutsu to Ninjutsu
By Shigetsu Doshi

What is Ninjutsu?
By Fujita Seiko

Koryu Bujutsu

by Sugawara Sadamoto

The Complete Martial Arts of Japan Volume One: Gekken
The Complete Martial Arts of Japan Volume Two: Jujutsu
The Complete Martial Arts of Japan Volume Three: Kenbu

Bokuden Ryu Jujutsu
By Otsuka Nobuyoshi

Heiho Yukan Volumes 17~20
with Kazuhiro Iida

The Sword Scroll
By Yamamoto Kansuke with Fumio Manaka

The Police Officers' Essential Illustrated Guide to Kenpo
By Tetsutaro Hisatomi

Fudochi Shin Myoroku: The Mysterious Record of Immovable Wisdom
By Takuan Soho with Fumio Manaka

Seppuku
By Uemon Moridan with Fumio Manaka

Self-Defense for Women
By Nohata Showa

Bojutsu: The Matsumoto System
By Matsumoto Torata

BOJUTSU: THE MATSUMOTO SYSTEM 松本式棒術

Notes about this translation:

This book was written in 1926 by a man named Matsumoto Torata. He likely worked as a teacher in the city of Nagasaki. Matsumoto Sensei was one of many people who attempted to reformat Koryu Bujutsu into something that could be incorporated in schools.

The original book was laid out somewhat awkwardly with the pictures of one technique beside the description of a different technique. Also many of the explanations require that you have to flip back to earlier sections of the book. To make it easier to follow, I have arranged the text and images for each chapter so they correspond. Also, whenever a chapter refers to a previous chapter, that information and corresponding picture are reproduced in order to make it easier to envision the entire technique.

In conclusion, while the book is reproduced in its entirety the layout has been changed from the original. Text has been moved and pictures that were reproduced only once have been added as dictated by the author's text. The Japanese version of each technique is presented first and the translation follows.

This book was translated for the purpose of research into how Japanese martial arts transitioned from techniques taught to Samurai for war into arts used to strengthen the mind and spirit in times of peace.

MATSUMOTO TORATA 松本寅太

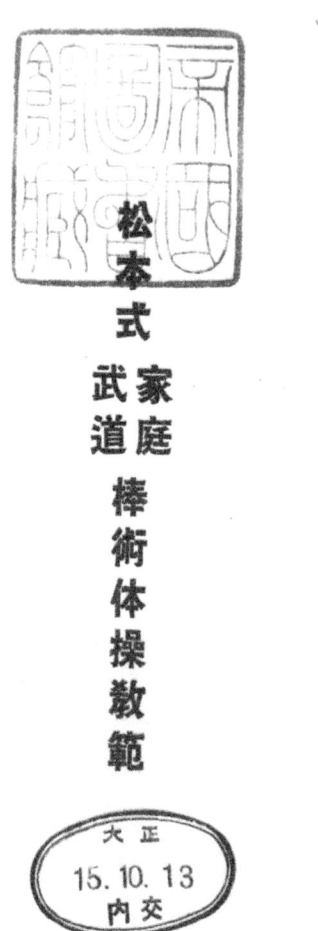

Practical Martial Arts
The Matsumoto System

An Instructor's Handbook to Bojutsu
Exercises

恩師 島袋美賢先生

創始者 松本寅太

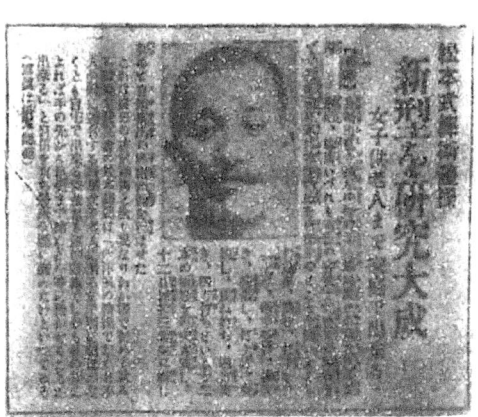

Top Left: My revered teacher Tejima Bishitsu.
* Note: Tejima Bishitsu was a practitioner of the Shingyoto Muto Ryu 心形刀無刀流 of swordfighting. The only information I could find on him is that in 1900 he received a *Seiren Sho* or Certificate of Supreme Talent at the Fifth Annual Martial Arts Demonstration held by the Butokukai, a martial arts organization. The demo/ competition was held annually from 1895-1932.

Bottom Left: Founder Matsumoto Torata.
* Note: Absolutely no additional information.

The top and bottom right newspaper clippings are form the Osaka Daily Newspaper, Western Daily, Kyushu Edition. The article is titled,

Matsumoto Style Bojutsu: Research into a new Style a Great success. A practical method that can be practiced by boys and girls young and old alike!

The rest of the article is unfortunately illegible.

長崎市月見町二丁目
術棒園年少

架 休 術 棒　　校學中星海市崎長

Top picture: Youth group practicing Bojutsu in Tomachi Nichome in Nagasaki City

Bottom picture: Students of Kaisei Junior High School Drilling Bojutsu Exercises.

Note: Kaisei Junior High School, which was founded in 1892 is still around today. The current structure dates from 1947.

棒術体操を學ぶ人のために

創始者　松本寅太

棒術は古來我が國の特技で忠孝敬神、所謂國民精神を基礎として吾人の精神、膽力を練磨する上において、他の武道と何等異なるところがないのであります。しかし今ここに私が提唱せんとするこの棒術体操においては、武道としての深い理論を抜きにして、たゞ棒術が他の武術と異なる一二の點を述べて見たいと思ひます。

棒術は攻擊殺人を主とする武術でなく、兇器を持つ敵に直面した場合一個の棒を以てこれを制し、または有り合せの棒ぎれを手にして敵を防ぐといふ、眞に意義ある正當の護身術であるといつても差支へありません。

だから昔日の所謂棒術は決して戰時用でなく、かの柔術等と共に捕繩術或は生捕術として盛に練磨されたものであります。しかるに現今では柔道の如き時勢に適應した武道であり、かつ体育上効果あるものとして他の武道を凌いで盛んにこれが練習を

To Those Seeking to Learn About Exercising With Bojutsu
By The Founder, Matsumoto Torata

* Bo= A wooden staff
* Bojutsu= Techniques for fighting or defending with a wooden staff

The Japanese have been adept at Bojutsu, the art of fighting with a wooden staff, from days long past. Loyalty and reverence, the foundations of our national identity, are therefore deeply ingrained into it. Training with the Bo is no different than practicing any other martial art. It strengthens the mind and forges strong nerves. What I am advocating with Bujojutsu-Taiso, or Staff Exercise program, first requires us to place the deeper philosophical and theoretical aspects of this martial art aside and highlight two points that differentiate this martial art from the others.

Bojutsu is not a typical offensive or killing weapon, instead this simple stick can be used to subdue an opponent armed with some sort of dangerous implement. Further, you could even pick up a broken piece of wood that was lying about and defend yourself against an attacker. There is no comparable method of self-defense as legitimate and versatile as Bojutsu.

Even long ago the techniques that comprise Bojutsu were not used as weapons of war, but were frequently trained in conjunction with Hojoutsu, the art of tying someone up with rope, and Ikegojutsu, the art of capturing someone alive. Moreover, much like Judo, it is a martial art in step with the times. The health benefits of Bojutsu surpass those of any other martial art thereby increasing your motivation to continue with training. Nowadays all that remains of Bojutsu are the Kata, or pre-determined sets of movements and strikes that are extensively trained by only a smaller number of expert martial arts practitioners.

續けられてゐます。が棒術は今日では型のみ存し、その型なるものも一部の武道專門家の間に習熟されてゐるのみで、勝負術、体育法として學ぶものは極めて稀であります。これは敎授の任に當る適任者が得難いといふことに原因してゐるかも知れませんが――わたくし共の見るところでは、この棒術は決して時代後れの武術でなく、否却つて無刀術を學ぶ人と否とを問はず、一般國民の習得しおくべき國技といつても過言ではなからうと信じます。

この棒術に使用する棒は長棒一名六尺棒、乳切木杖、短棒といふやうな各種類があり、かつまた塲合によつては有合せの棒切を以て不時の迫害を防禦することも出來ます。尤も乳切木杖の實用武器は各自の身長と技倆によつてその長さを定められ、一方には三寸五分の槍を藏し、一方には鎖を以てし敵に對するのであります。しかして棒術は各種とも殺敵、生捕の二法によるものでありますから、平時太平の武術として、自衞護身術として最適當のものと思ひます。また私はこの術を体操化し朝夕の家庭体操としてもその型は確かに体育の目的を達する上に上々の術であると思料します。しか

二

The Matsumoto System gives you the opportunity to learn this rare and extraordinary method to refine your body and understand how to defeat an opponent in combat.

No doubt I feel this way because I found it so difficult to learn this material well enough to pass it on but... from where I stand Bojutsu is absolutely not some dusty anachronistic martial art. First of all, it is clearly an art that should be studied by those interested in Mutodori, or fighting without a sword (against an opponent with a sword). However, it would also not be an exaggeration to say that these techniques that have been passed down over many generations are something that should be embraced by the general populace as well.

The Bo used for this Bojutsu is fairly long. Each person trains with what is known as a Rokushaku Bo (one Shaku is approximately 30cm. Total length is 180cm.) Other varieties of staff like Chigiriki (Staff with chain or blade attached) and the Han-Bo (Half-staff) are also used. The reason for this is that when suddenly attacked you may have to employ whatever broken piece of stick that is around to defend yourself from harm.

Originally the Chigiriki was a practical weapon that was sized according to the height and ability of the user. Some would have a spearhead 3 Sun 5 Bun (10cm) long on the end while others would use a chain to face an opponent. With Bojutsu you have at your disposal two methods: One is Satteki, or strikes to kill the enemy, and the other is Seiho, or restraining and capturing techniques. Therefore I feel that in these tranquil times Bojutsu is eminently suited for self-protection and self-defense.

What I have done with this book is to develop a practical form of exercise utilizing the Bo that can be done morning and night.

棒はかの劍、槍、弓などの如く一方に偏せない武器であるから、したがつて全身的に活動することによつて、心身共に鍛鍊の實をあぐることが出來ます。かつ自衞の一助とすると共に家庭における老幼男女に對し少しも無理がなく各その人の體質に應じて、一人でも三人でも僅か二三分間のうちに行ふことが出來ます。

The methods I present will enable you to achieve a higher level of physical fitness as you achieve proficiency in these techniques. It is important realize that the staff is not a one sided weapon like the sword, the spear or firing arrows. Using the Bo requires you to activate your entire body therefore strengthening your frame and focusing your mind.

This school of self-defense can be practiced at home by young and old, men and women each according to their ability and without undo strain. It can be practiced solo or in groups of two or three. The entire training regimen can be done in under three minutes.

* Note: The Chigiriki, written as either 契木 Karma Stick or somewhat more humorously as 乳切木 which translates to "cut off at the nipple wood." This references the fact that the ideal height of this weapon was said to be at your nipple so that is where you cut the wood (though it could also be made of bamboo). It typically has a chain on the end of it though this author states a spearhead is also possible. The illustration below from the Edo period *Two Hundred Illustrations of Weapons* 武器皕図 shows it third from the left grouped with other similar weapons.

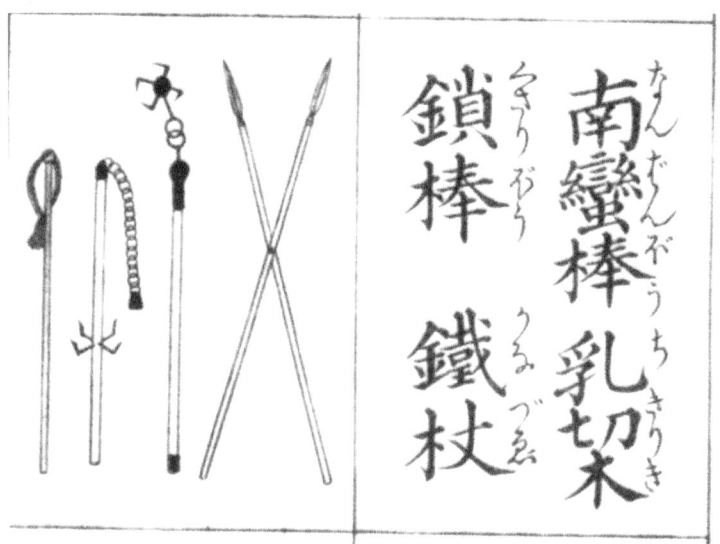

練習に取かゝる前に

一、棒術体操は團体々操、家庭体操として行ふ場合一個の棒以外一切何等の用具を要せぬ。

一、棒は大体において長さ四尺二三寸、直徑八分乃至八分五厘程度で女子供用は適誼である。

一、團体的に行ふ場合は向合せに打合ふのが最も宜しい。

一、技を行ふ場合は、自分の前に敵が直面してゐるとの假想を以て對すること。

一、体操に用ふる懸聲は左の三種である。

Before Beginning Training

- These Bojutsu Exercise were designed as a practical method for training at home. All that is required to begin training is a Bo.

- The Bo you prepare should be about four Shaku and two or three Sun in length (152-153cm) with a diameter of about eight Bun to eight Bun and five Rin (3.1-3.2cm) so that girls can easily use it as well.

- The best way to train is in a group with all members facing each other as they strike.

- When training you should imagine that the enemy is directly in front of you.

- The Kake-Goe, or vocalizations paired with actions are as listed on the following page:

やー。ゑい。とー。而して懸聲は第一元氣を旺盛ならしめ、第二技術動作を敏活にし、第三腹部の力を強むる等、所謂三德があるもので、武道の蘊奧たる氣合術も實にこの懸聲が中心生命となつてゐるから、十分腹部に力を入れ大聲に元氣あろ強い聲をもてかくることに努めねばならぬ。

一、演技中は如何なる場合を問はず常に誠心誠意を以て當り特に始と終に行ふ禮儀は極めて正しく行ふこと。

一、指揮者は氣をつけ、禮、用意、始め、終り、等の號令を發し必要の場合一二三等と呼稱して技術の進行をはかること。

一、整列時人と人との間隔は棒を一方横に出し傍の人に觸れざるやう、また前後は打合に支障なき間隔をとること。

一、型は一ケ年を形どり第一打込み（忠）第二拂ひ（孝）第三打下し（天）第四拂上げ（地）第五兩手受け（人）第六拂突き（仁）第七拂落し（義）第八打上げまたは返し突き（禮）第九受流し（智）第十重ね打ち（信）第十一四方突き（陰）第十二四方打ち（陽）の

- Ya! Ei! Toh! The three Toku, or benefits, of using Kake-Goe as you train are first, it pumps you full of vim and vigor. Second, it makes your movement more precise. Third, it places power in your abdomen.

    A deep inner teaching of Budo, or martial arts, is Kiaijutsu. Kiaijutsu is the use of vocalizations to sharpen the mind, heal the spirit or heal the body. Clearly, Kakegoe is a fundamental and vital part of Kiaijutsu. You should make a concerted effort to put power in your abdomen as you vocalize loud, enthusiastic Kake-Goe.

- Always fully commit your mind and body to training and endeavor to remain focused throughout. In particular the bow at the beginning and end should be crisp and proper.

- The instructor should provide vocal commands such as Rei! (bow), Yoi! (prepare), Hajime! (begin) and Owari! (end). In addition to this, commands such as counting Ichi, Ni, San (1,2,3) can be added as necessary as you proceed through the program.

- When practicing in a line be sure there is a sufficient interval between practitioners. Each person should extend their Bo out to the side ensuring it does not touch another person. Also make sure there is enough space in front and behind so strikes can be done freely.

- There are twelve Kata, or sets of strikes, just as there are twelve months in a year.

1. Uchi-Komi: Move in and Strike.
   Known by the Kanji 忠 *Chu-* **Loyalty**.
2. Harai: Sweeping Strike.
   Known by the Kanji 孝 *Ko-* **Filial Piety**.
3. Uchi Oroshi: Downward Strike.
4. Known by the Kanji 天 *Ten-* **Heaven**.
5. Harai Age: Rising Sweeping Strike.
   Known by the Kanji 地 *Chi-* **Earth**.
6. Ryo-te Uke: Receiving a Strike With Both Hands.
   Known by the Kanji 人 *Hito-* **Human.**
7. Harai Tsuki: Sweeping Strike to Stab.
   Known by the Kanji 仁 *Nin-* **Benevolence**.
8. Harai Otoshi: Decending Sweeping Strike.
   Known by the Kanji 義 *Gi-* **Justice**.
9. Uchi Age: Lifting Strike. Also referred to as Kaeshi Uchi: Returning a Strike.
   Known by the Kanji 礼 *Rei-* **Respect**.
10. Uke Nagashi: Receive and Pass.
    Known by the Kanji 智 *Chi-* **Wisdom**.
11. Kasane Uchi: Repeated Strikes.
    Known by the Kanji 信 *Shin-* **Trust**.
12. Shiho Tsuki: Four Way Stabbing Strike.
    Known by the Kanji 陰 *In-* **Moon**.
13. Shiho Uchi: Four Way Strike.
    Known by the Kanji 陽 *Yo-* **Sun**.

Note: The twelve Kata are each represented by one Kanji. The words are arranged in a mnemonic device consisting of common Japanese words. The first two Kanji form Chuko, a word that combines of Loyalty and Fealty. The second three words heaven earth and human form the word Tenchijin, a word that means everything that makes up the universe. The next five Benevolence, Justice, Respect, Wisdom and Trust are together referred to as the Five Virtues, a concept originating in Confucianism. The final two In and Yo have many meanings including the Yin and Yang duality, darkness and light, male and female but I chose Moon and Sun.

十二本より成る。
一、左記解説は左右兩術同一のものにつき重複の煩をさげ右の場合のみをとり、特種の技術は左右共に解説を試みてある。
一、家庭武術として練磨なす場合對手には棒或は木太刀等を持たせて練習すべし。

棒を以て直し立たする圖

- The techniques written on the previous page are done the same way on both the left and right sides. Repeating the instructions for both the left and right sides would be redundant so only the right side will be explained. Some techniques may require extra description for both the left and right sides.

- When training at home the opponent should be armed with either a Bo or a Ki-Dachi wooden sword.

Illustration of the Bo being held vertically.

* Note: There are several words that refer to a wooden sword including:

Ki-Dachi 木太刀
Bokken 木劍
Bokkto 木刀

The words all basically refer to the same thing, a piece of wood shaped into a sword but the length, shape and weight as well as the type of wood used can vary from school to school.

一本目 打込み(忠)

用意　右足を後方に引き(この距離約一尺)体を斜に右手を上に伸し左手は顔面右方に第一圖の如くなす。

一、右足を左足に寄すると同時に左足を後方に前同様引くと同時に両手にて第二圖の如く右方より敵の面上に打込む。

二、打込みたる左手を後方高く上げこの間棒より指の離れざるやう取換へ前同様左方より敵の面上に打込む。

(忠)

打込の其一

Chu Loyalty

(忠)

打込の其二

Uchi Komi- Move in and Strike

Illustration Two

First Technique

Uchi Komi- Move in and Strike

Represented by the Kanji 忠 Chu: Loyalty

Preparation

Pull the right foot back (this distance should be about one Shaku or 30cm) and turn your body diagonally. Stretch your right arm above you. Your left hand should be level with the right side of your face. See the first illustration.

Step One

You attack by bringing the Bo down with both hands while sliding your right foot forward and, at the same time, bringing the left foot backwards. Draw your left foot back the same way the right foot was pulled back at the beginning.

The attack, which you have launched from your right side, should strike the top of the opponent's head. See the second illustration.

Step Two

Lift the Bo back and up high with your left hand. Do not allow your fingers to release the Bo. With the hands now reversed, strike to the top of the opponent's head the same way as before, but this time the attack is from left side.

二本目 拂ひ（孝）

用意　左手にて棒の先端を握る、その際左手母指の下方に向き右足を後方に引き第一圖の如き姿勢をとる。

一、右足を左足に引寄せ同時に右手にて敵の脛部を拂ふ心持にて第二圖の如き姿勢をつくる。

（孝）

Koh: Fealty

(孝)

Sweeping Strike

Illustration Two

二、左手にて棒を後に引下げ第一圖の反對左の方より前同樣敵の脛部を拂ふ。

Second Technique

Harai-Sweeping Strike

Represented by the Kanji 孝 Koh: Fealty

Preparation

Grip the very end of the Bo with your left hand. When doing this the thumb of your left hand should be facing down. Pull your right foot back. You should be positioned as shown in the first illustration.

Step One

Step forward with your right foot as you pull your left foot back. At the same time move the Bo in a sweeping motion with your right hand, envisioning striking the enemy in the shin. You should end up positioned as shown in the second illustration.

* Note: The pictures in the book are mislabeled and in the wrong order, it has been corrected here.

Step Two

Pull the Bo behind you with your left hand so that you end up in the opposite stance of the first illustration. Next, from this stance do a sweeping strike to the enemy's shin starting from your left side.

三本目 打下し（天）

用意　一本目と同じ。

一、敵わが面上に向つて勢よく斬下し來るときわが右足を右方この間一尺に踏み体を開き直りて左の足を後方に引き空を打たせ敵の脛部を横或は後部より圖の如く打下す。

二、左方に体を轉じ前同様にすべし。

Ten: Heaven

（天）

打下したる所

Position after the downward strike

Third Technique

Uchi Oroshi- Downward Strike

Represented by the Kanji 天 Ten: Heaven

Preparation

Begin this technique the same as the first technique.

[Pull the right foot back (this distance should be about one Shaku or 30cm) and turn your body diagonally. Stretch your right arm above you. Your left hand should be level with the right side of your face.]

* Note: The brackets [] indicate information is repeated.

Step One

In this technique the opponent is driving full-force directly at you, intending to cut straight down on top of your head. In response to this attack step out with your right foot about one Shaku.

To completely take your body off the line of attack, pull your left foot back placing your body diagonal to the opponent. This means the opponent only cuts air. Strike down onto the side or back of the opponent's shin as shown in the illustration.

Step Two

Turn your body to the left and repeat the technique starting from the other side.

四本目 拂上げ（地）

用意　二本目と同じ。

一、三本目と同じく体を開き下方より上に圖の如く敵の頭部を打ちまたは太刀を拂ふ動作をなす。

二、これまた三本目同様体を開き拂上げること右と同じ。

Chi : Earth

（地）

拂上げたる所

Position after the rising, sweeping strike

Fourth Technique

Harai Age- Rising Sweeping Strike

Represented by the Kanji 地 Chi: Earth

Preparation

Begin this technique the same as the first technique.

[Grip the very end of the Bo with your left hand. When doing this the thumb of your left hand should be facing down. Pull your right foot back.]

Step One

Just as in the third technique, open your body to the side when the opponent strikes. Sweep up from below with a sweeping motion either to the opponent's head or to his sword. This will knock away the sword opponent's sword.

Step Two

This step also follows the pattern of the third technique. Open your body up to the other side and strike from the left side in the same manner.

五本目　兩手受け（人）

用意　棒を第一圖の如く前方にとる。

一、右足を後方に引きこの時右足の膝關接を曲げ右手を十分後に伸し第二回の如くなす。

二、敵の振上げし太刀を打下し來らざるうちに右足を前に第三圖の如く勢よく兩手を受止む。

三、握りし棒をそのまゝ第一圖の如く復す。また左に移るときは棒は左方に譲り右と同様になす。この技は最も思ひ切りたる入身の術にて強くこの型にはまるときは敵は後方に轉倒するものである。

Hito: Human

Illustration One of Ryote Uke
Receiving a Blow With Two Hands

Hito: Human

(人)

二其け受手両

Illustration Two of Ryote Uke
Receiving a Blow With Two Hands

Hito: Human

(人)

三其け受手両

Illustration Three of Ryote Uke
Receiving a Blow With Two Hands

Fifth Technique

Ryote Uchi- Receiving a Blow With Both Hands

Represented by the Kanji 人 Hito: Human

Preparation

Hold the Bo in front of you as shown in the first illustration.

Step One

Pull your right foot back. When doing this make sure your right knee is bent and your right arm is extended back fully. Your position should look like illustration two.

Step Two

Before the opponent has a chance to finish their downward sword strike, launch yourself forward with your right foot, as the third illustration shows. Receive and stop the blow with both arms extended.

Step Three

While still holding the Bo with both hands return to the position shown in the first illustration.

When doing this technique on the left side, draw the Bo back to the left instead of to the right. Other than that it is done in the same manner as on your right side.

* Note: Picture reversed.

The first movement in this technique is Irimi Jutsu which means moving your body towards the opponent. In this case you are launching your body directly at the opponent the moment the attack begins. This Irimi requires you to fully commit to this technique. The force of your entry will result in the attacker being thrown backwards onto the ground.

六本目 拂ひ突き（仁）

用意　左足を後方に棒の先を地上二三寸に下げ第一圖の如き姿勢をとる。この時右膝關節を少し曲げる。

一 其突拂

一、敵が面上に斬下すとき われは右手を十分上の方に伸べ体を少く後方に第二圖の如き姿勢にて敵の太刀を左方に拂ふ。

二、左足を前に廣く踏出すと共に左手を上の方へ伸べ左手を緩く右手は強く握り右手を左手の掌まで第三圖の如く伸ばし敵の胸部を突く。

三、右手を後方へ引くと共に左足を引き直立となる。此時棒の先を下げ次に左の方に移る時は用意の姿勢と同一の行動を一時に行ひ他は右と同じ。

Nin: Benevolence
(仁)

一 其 突 拂

Harai Tsuki- Sweeping Strike and Stab

Illustration One

Nin: Benevolence

(仁)

拂 突 其 二

Harai Tsuki- Sweeping Strike and Stab

Illustration Two

Nin: Benevolence

(仁)

拂突其三

Harai Tsuki- Sweeping Strike and Stab

Illustration Three

Sixth Technique

Harai Tsuki- Sweeping Strike and Stab

Represented by the Kanji 仁 Nin: Benevolence

Preparation

Place your left foot behind you. Lower the end of your Bo so that it is two or three Sun, 6~9cm, above the ground. Your stance should look like what is shown in the first illustration. Your right knee should be slightly bent at this point.

Step One

As the opponent begins a downward cut, aiming for the top of your head, pull the Bo upward as you rock your body slightly backwards. See the second illustration. The opponent's sword should be swept to the left by this action.

Step Two

Step forward deeply with your left foot and bring your left hand up and forward. When doing this switching movement neither the left nor the right hand should release the Bo.

The left hand holds the Bo gently while the right hand grips it firmly. Thrust the Bo forward with your right hand until it connects with the palm of your left hand. See the third illustration.

Step Three

Pull your right hand back as you draw your left foot back. You will return to a standing position. From there, lower the end of the Bo and do the technique from the left side. Before beginning the technique on the other side, return to the ready position and pause. Other than that, the movements are exactly the same as on the right hand side.

七本目　拂ひ落し（義）

用意　五本目に同じ。

一、右足を前に胸部を張り棒を第一圖の如く後頭部から両肩に擔ひ十分敵の行動に注意し敵がわが胴または脛部に斬付けんとして來るとき。

二、われは右足を後に引き体を引くと同時に左手を棒より移し右手にて敵の太刀を打拂ふ。この時左手は第二圖の如く棒を握る。

三、左手に持ちたる棒を右方に押し右手の先をとり用意の時の姿勢となる左は同じ

Gi: Justice

(義)

一 其 し 落 拂

Harai Otoshi- Dropping Sweep Strike

Illustration One

Gi: Justice

Harai Otoshi- Dropping Sweep Strike

Illustration Two

Seventh Technique

Harai Otoshi- Dropping Sweep Strike

Represented by the Kanji 義 Gi: Duty

Preparation

This technique begins the same way as the fifth technique.

[Hold the Bo in front of you as shown in the first illustration.]

Step One

With your right foot forward and the chest expanded outward, hold the Bo behind the head and across the shoulders. See the first illustration.

* Note: This stance makes you seem vulnerable and invites the opponent to strike.

You should be concentrating on watching for when the opponent launches a cut at either your waist or shin.

Step Two

When the attack comes, pull your right leg back and twist your torso to the right. At the same time release the Bo with your left hand. Swing it with your right hand to strike and sweep away the opponent's sword. At the end of the strike the left hand should grip the Bo as shown in illustration two.

Step Three

Return to the starting position by pulling the Bo with your left hand. Switch you right hand so it is positioned as shown in the starting position. The left side is done the same way.

八本目 打上げ（返し突き）（禮）

用意　直立して氣を付けそのまゝの姿勢。

一、右足、棒ともに後に引き左手を十分に伸ばしわが頭上を越ね第一圖の如く棒を握る。

二、勢よく彼我の棒と太刀が打合ひたる時敵は急ぎ太刀を上段に打込まんとする。

三、右足を後に第二圖の如き姿勢にて第三圖の如く右手にて敵が打下さんとする瞬間敵の顔面を突く。

四、右足を引き棒は左の方に立て再び左の業に移る便に備ふ。

（禮）

返し突き其一

Tai: Body

(禮)

返し突き其二

Uchi Age- Strike and Force Upward
Also Known As
Kaeshi Tsuki: Return and Stab
Illustration Two

Tai Body

(禮)

返し突き其三

Uchi Age- Strike and Force Upward
Also Known As
Kaeshi Tsuki: Return and Stab
Illustration Three

Eighth Technique

Uchi Age- Strike and Force Upward

Also Known As

Kaeshi Tsuki: Return and Stab

Represented by the Kanji 体/體: Body

Preparation

This technique starts from standing at attention.

Step One

Pull back your right foot and the Bo at the same time. Ensure your left arm is stretched back fully and extends over your head.

Hold the Bo as shown in the first illustration.

Step Two

In this technique the opponent is attacking from Daijodan, a stance with the sword held above the head. The opponent is seeking to attack with great force and strike down before you can move your Bo.

Step Three

Keeping your right foot behind you, shift your stance to the position shown in the second illustration.

The third illustration shows how to use your right hand to thrust the end of the Bo into the opponent's face. This should be done the second they launch their attack.

Step Four

Pull your right foot back and bring the Bo to your left side. Return to the starting position holding the Bo vertically, but on your left side. You are not ready to do the technique on the left hand side.

Chi: Wisdom

九本目　受け流し（智）

用意　七本目に同じ。

一、敵われを一打にせんと一氣に飛込み打下し來る時われは棒を第一圖の如く面上に上げ左足を左前斜に飛開き棒の端を左の方にて太刀を受け流す。

二、行き過ぎたる敵を第二圖の如き要領にて突く。

三、用意の姿勢に戻る、左も亦同じ。

別法　第一圖の如く飛開きたる刹那左の方の棒

（智）

一　受け流し其一

Uke Nagashi- Receive and Strike

Illustration One

Chi: Wisdom

(智)

の端にて敵の后頭部を強打するもよし。

受し流し其二

Uke Nagashi- Receive and Strike

Illustration Two

Ninth Technique

Uke Nagashi- Receive and Strike

Represented by the Kanji 知 Chi: Wisdom

Preparation

This technique begins the same way as the seventh technique.

[Hold the Bo in front of you as shown in the first illustration.]

* Note: While not stated explicitly, the opponent is standing directly in front of you.

Step One

The opponent is looking for an opportunity to launch a strike. Seeing one, the opponent leaps in and swings downward. At that moment you should bring your Bo up and step rapidly with your left foot diagonally. This opens the body up as shown in the illustration.

The opponent's sword should glance off the [right] end of the Bo and pass by.

Step Two

Stab the Bo to the face of the opponent who has cut only air with their strike. The attack should be as shown in the second illustration.

Step Three

Return to the starting position. The left side is done the same way.

Another Method To Do The Same Technique

The second that you launch yourself diagonally forward, strike hard to the back of the opponent's head with the left end of the Bo.

十本目 重ね打ち（信）

一、用意 棒の先を敵の顔面に第一圖の如く構ふ。敵の顔面を突く動作をなす。

二、左手を後方に高く右手よりすぐき上げ左足を前方に踏出すとともに左手を前に第二圖の如き姿勢にて打ちかゝる。

三、兩足ともそのまゝに右手にて棒をすぐき後方高く上げると同時に打込む。

四、棒より左手を放し棒先を下方に廻轉せしめ右脇下に棒を狹み左足を引き第三圖の如き姿勢をとる。左は一にて用意および一の動作を一時になす。ほか右と同じ

（信）

重打ち其一

Shin: Trust
Kasane Uchi- Multiple Strikes
Illustration One

Shin: Trust

(信)

重ち打其二

Kasane Uchi- Multiple Strikes

Illustration Two

Shin: Trust

(信)

三 其 ち 打 重

Kasane Uchi- Multiple Strikes

Illustration Three

Tenth Technique

Kasane Uchi- Multiple Strikes

Represented by the Kanji 信 Shin: Trust

Preparation

You should position the Bo so that the end is pointing at the opponent's face. See the first illustration.

Step One

Do a stabbing thrust, or Tsuki, to the opponent's face.

* Note: This means you would push the Bo with the left hand forward until it meets the palm of the right hand.

Step Two

Raise the Bo up high behind you with your left hand. The right hand holds loosely, allowing the Bo to slide through your fingers. Step forward with your left foot and, at the same time, bring the left hand forward so that you strike as shown in the second illustration.

Step Three

Keeping both feet in that position, raise the Bo behind you with the right hand and allow it to slide through your left. As soon as you bring it up, strike.

* Note: Since the feet stay in place you are twisting the hips forward as you strike.

Step Four

Release the Bo with your left hand and allow the tip of the Bo to drop as you spin the Bo around so that it stops under your right armpit. After pinning it with your armpit, pull your left foot back. Your body should be positioned as shown in the third illustration. Before starting the technique with the left hand forward, return to the initial position and pause. Do the Tsuki. Everything else is the same as when your right hand is initially forward.

十一本目 四方突き（陰）

用意　九本目に同じ。

注意　この技は前後に敵を受けたる時われは前進と見せ不意に後方の敵を突き一人對敵爲す型である。

一、圖の如く後方を突く。

二、後方に引きたる右足を前に出し棒も亦同じく前方を突く。

三、右足を右に開き棒も亦十分兩手を伸ばして右を突く（棒は後方突端にて）

四、右足と左足より左の方へ出し棒も亦左方を突く。

五、元の姿勢にかへりて右の同じ様に移る。

後なる突たる所

In: Moon

Shiho Tsuki- Stabbing Strike in Four Directions
The illustration shows the stab to the back.

Eleventh Technique

Shiho Tsuki- Stabbing Strike in Four Directions

Represented by the Kanji 陰 In: Moon (Yin)

Preparation

This technique begins the same way as the ninth technique.

[Hold the Bo in front of you as shown in the first illustration.]

* Note: While not stated explicitly, the opponent is standing directly in front of you.

Caution

This technique envisions attackers both in front and behind you. In this situation you pretend to have all your attention focused on the enemy in front of you, then suddenly stab the Bo at the attacker behind you. The technique is attacking each of these opponents in turn.

Step One

Stab backwards with your Bo as the first illustration shows.

Step Two

Step forward with your right leg that you had drawn back for the first strike. At the same time, stab forward in the same way you stabbed backwards.

Step Three

Step out to the right with your right foot. Extend both arms out fully, then stab with the Bo to the right. The strike should be with the back of the Bo.

Step Four

Just as you stepped out to the right with the right foot, step out to the left and stab with the end of the Bo.

Step Five

Return to the starting position and do the technique again starting on your left side.

十二本目 四方打ち（陽）

注意　この技は十一本目と連續的の技である各技を綴り合せたる技であるから一本目と共に棒の手さばきの大体と見てよろしい。

用意　右向となり一本目の如く右足を左足後方に引く。

一二まで一本目に同じ

三四また二本目に同じ

異なる點々たゞ棒の端を握る手が上下打込み拂ひの連續に便なるやう第二圖の如く握る。

五、再び上段にとり一本打込む。

六、敵を突きそのまゝ

（陽）

下段な打たる所 Yo: Sun

The illustration shows how the lower strike should be done

た一にて左の方向より後向きとなり前同様一より六まで行ひ、この度は左向ひに一より六まで同様に行ひ、更に左の方向より後向となり一より六まで打込みて技は終る。この時四方を濟ましたる体は最初の方向になつておらねばならぬ。

Twelfth Technique

Shiho Uchi- Striking in Four Directions

Represented by the Kanji 陽 Yo: Sun (Yang)

Caution

This technique is a continuation of the eleventh technique. All the movements from the previous eleven techniques are included. It would therefore be prudent to review the movements and the way the Bo is handled.

Preparation

This technique begins the same as the first technique. The opponent is on your right hand side. Pull your right foot back about one Shaku, 30cm, behind your left foot. Stretch your right arm above you. Your left hand should be level with the right side of your face.

Step One

Steps one and two are also the same as the first technique. You attack by bringing the Bo down with both hands while sliding your right foot forward and, at the same time, bringing the left foot backwards.

The attack, which you have launched from your right side, should strike the top of the opponent's head. See the second illustration.

Step Two

Lift the Bo back and up high with your left hand. Do not allow your fingers to release the Bo. With the hands now reversed, strike to the top of the opponent's head the same way as before, but this time from the attack is from left side.

Steps Three and Four

These two steps are the same as steps one and two of the second technique.

After finishing the second strike to the head in step two, bring the Bo behind you gripping the end of the Bo with your left hand. When doing this the thumb of your left hand should be facing down. Pull your right foot back. You should be positioned as shown in the illustration at left.

Step forward with your right foot as you pull your left foot back. At the same time move the Bo in a sweeping motion with your right hand, envisioning striking the enemy in the shin. The only difference in steps three and four is the positioning of the back hand. It should be changed from the position in the left picture to the one on the right. This makes the flow of upper and lower strikes smoother.

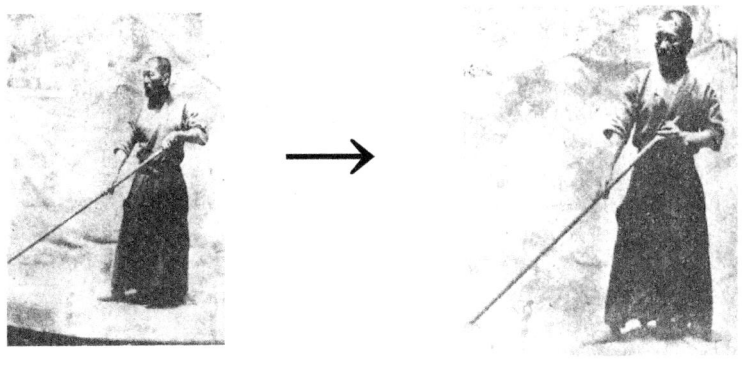

Use your left hand to pull the Bo behind you so that you end up in the opposite stance of the first illustration. Next, from this stance do a sweeping strike to the enemy's shin starting from your left side.

Step Five

Return to Jodan no Kamae and strike the top of the opponent's head with your right hand forward.

Step Six

The fifth step ended with the Bo striking the opponent on the head. Keeping the Bo in that position, rotate your body to the left until you are facing the opposite direction. You have now returned to the starting position with the Bo above your head.

Next repeat steps one through six again, this time with your left hand leading. Having finished that, again turn left to face behind you and do steps one through six.

By the end of Striking in Four Directions you should be facing the same way you started.

* Note: Shiho's literal meaning is "four directions" but it can mean "many directions" or "all directions." The Bo is moving in many directions though your body doesn't do the technique facing each of the four cardinal directions.

參考技

棒は太刀と異なり其の突端を敵に捕へられる事がある。其場合入身の法は幾多あるが其一二を舉げん。

一、敵に我が棒に一端を捕へ面上に向つて斬り付けんとする時、我は一圖の如き方法に依りこれを受止む。敵又下段を斬らむとする時我は右手を下に

（其一）
Illustration One

下げ二圖の如く飛び替はる。敵又棒を下に下げ面上に向つて來る時は三圖の如く入身さなつて右腕首にて敵の腕首を受け止め直に敵の腕を握ると共に左手を前に廻し右足を前に四圖の如く敵の右手をきめ付け又は組伏するのである。

（其 二）

Illustration Two

(其 三)

Illustration Three

MATSUMOTO TORATA 松本寅太

(其四)

Illustration Four

Additional Techniques

The Bo is different from a sword since the opponent can grab the end of it after a thrust. There are numerous ways to move your body to deal with this situation and I would like to present one or two of them here.

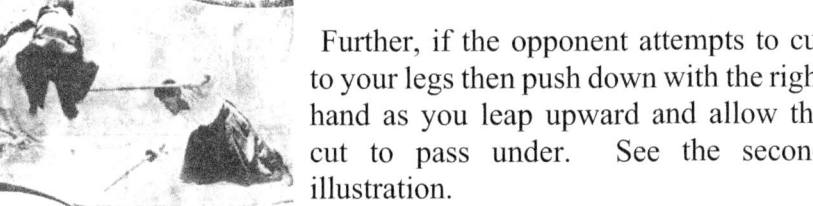

In this situation the opponent has grabbed one end of your Bo and is intent on cutting straight down on your head. You should move your body as shown in this illustration and block the attack.

Further, if the opponent attempts to cut to your legs then push down with the right hand as you leap upward and allow the cut to pass under. See the second illustration.

If the opponent then tries to lower the Bo and cut to the top of your head respond by moving your body as is shown in the third illustration.

Naga Bo　Illustration One

長　棒

長棒は其の中央を兩手に圖の如く握り棒の兩方を自由に活用す可きものとす。

（其　一）

Naga Bo Illustration Two

(二 其)

The Long Bo

When holding the Naga Bo or the Long Bo both of your hands should be in the center part of the Bo. By holding it here both ends of the Bo can be utilized in a fight.

* Note: Illustrations one and two have no additional information so they are likely just showing two different stances with the Naga Bo.

短　棒

短棒も受方入身等種々の法あるがここには簡單なる一例を記す。

敵面上より斬り下し來る時我は左足を敵の右橫に踏み込み我左手を高く一圖の如く受流すと同時に敵の柄と手の間に棒の手許を突き入れ左手を下に二圖の如く強く引く時は敵は太刀を落すか前にうつぶせに倒れるものである。

Illustration One

Illustration Two

Short Bo

Tan Bo, or the Short Bo is quite versatile. You can use it to block and receive strikes, move into the opponent's space and then attack. I will offer one simple example here.

The opponent attacks by cutting down at your head. As soon as this cut is launched you should step towards the opponent's right side. Raise your right hand as shown in the first illustration. This will allow the opponent's sword to slide off your Tan Bo in what is known as an Uke Nagashi, receive and pass. At the same time bring the Tan Bo down in a sharp strike on both of the opponent's wrists. This strike, which is basically aimed at the handle of the opponent's sword, should cause him to drop the sword and topple forward.

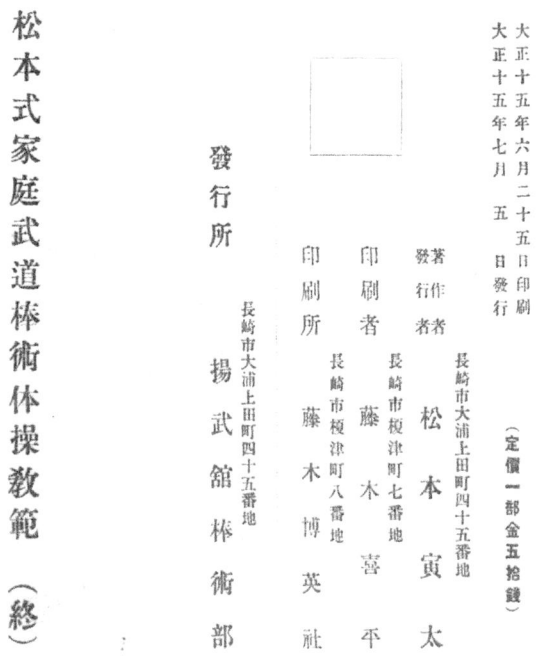

An Instructor's Handbook to The Matsumoto System Bojutsu Exercises

End

Published July 5, 1926
Written by Matsumoto Torata
A Publication of the Yobukan Bojutsu Club
Nagasaki, Japan

Printed in Great Britain
by Amazon